Romantic Hideaways

THOMAS KINKADE

HARVEST HOUSE PUBLISHERS
Eugene, Oregon 97402

ROMANTIC HIDEAWAYS

Copyright © 1997 Thomas Kinkade, Media Arts Group, Inc.
Published by Harvest House Publishers
Eugene, Oregon 97402

ISBN 1-56507-541-2

Media Arts Group, Inc.
521 Charcot Avenue
San Jose, CA 95131
1.800.366.3733

Design and production by:
Koechel Peterson & Associates
Minneapolis, Minnesota

97 98 99 00 01 02 03 04 05 06 /BP/ 10 9 8 7 6 5 4 3 2

It isn't good
for man
to be alone:
I will make
a companion
for him.

~ THE BOOK OF GENESIS

Come, my beloved,
let us go up
the shining mountain,
and sit together;
we will watch the sun
go down in beauty
from that shining place.

We will sit there
till the night traveler
rises in beauty above
the shining mountain;
we will watch him
as he climbs the skies.

We will watch also
the little stars
following their chief....

We sit in beauty, very still,
upon the shining mountain.

~ ABENAKI SONG

I never knew before, what such love
as you have made me feel, was;
I did not believe in it;
my Fanny, was afraid of it,
lest it should burn me up.
But if you will fully love me,
though there may be some fire
'twill not be more than we can bear . . .
I love you the more in that
I believe you have liked me
for my own sake and for nothing else.

~ JOHN KEATS TO FANNY BRAWNE

When the autumn

tinged the greenwood,

Turning all its leaves to gold,

In the lawn by the elders shaded,

I my love to Nellie told,

As we stood together, gazing

On the star-bespangled dome,

How I blessed the August evening,

When I saw sweet Nellie home.

~ TRADITIONAL SONG, 1858

"Seeing Nellie
Home"
Glee Club

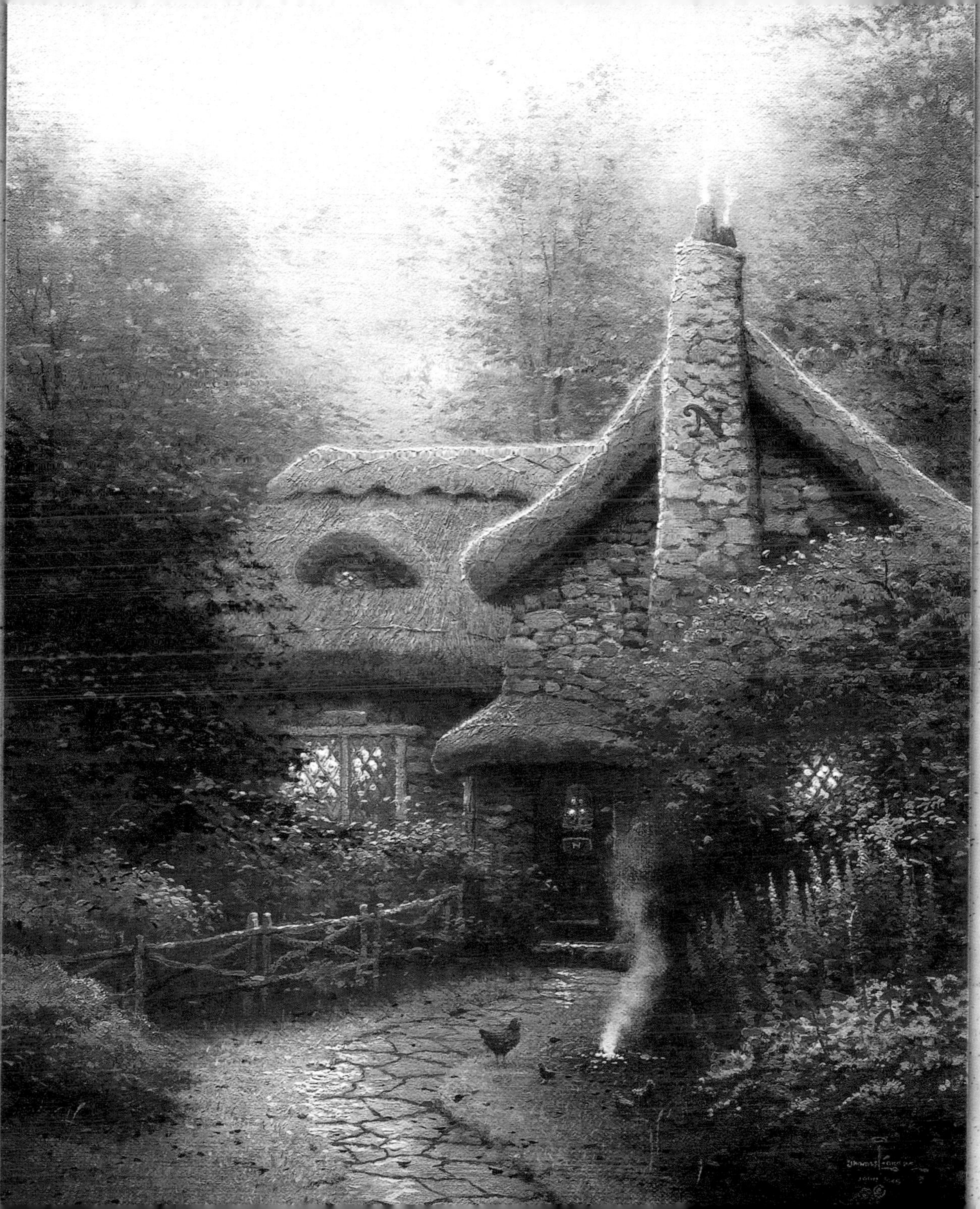

I know what it is to
live entirely for and with
what I love best on earth.
I hold myself supremely blest — blest
beyond what language can express;
because I am my husband's life
as fully as he is mine. No woman
was ever nearer to her mate than I am:
ever more absolutely bone of his bone,
and flesh of his flesh. I know no
weariness of my Edward's society:
he knows none of mine, any more
than we each do of the pulsation
of the heart that beats in our
separate bosoms; consequently,
we are ever together. To be together
is for us to be at once as free
as in solitude, as gay as in company.

~ CHARLOTTE BRONTË
JANE EYRE

E vidently she was

always going to understand;

she was always going to say the right thing.

The discovery made the cup of his bliss overflow,

and he went on gaily:

"The worst of it is that

I want to kiss you and I can't."

As he spoke he took a swift glance

about the conservatory,

assured himself of their momentary privacy,

and catching her to him laid

a fugitive pressure on her lips....

She sat silent, and the world lay

like a sunlit valley at their feet.

~ EDITH WHARTON
THE AGE OF INNOCENCE

*L*et him kiss me with the kisses of his mouth –

for your love is more delightful than wine.

Pleasing is the fragrance of your perfumes....

Take me away with you – let us hurry!

~ THE SONG OF SOLOMON

My spirits were excited,

and with pleasure and ease

I talked to him during supper,

and for a long time after.

There was no harassing restraint,

no repressing of glee and vivacity with him;

for with him I was at perfect ease,

because I knew I suited him:

all I said or did seemed

either to console or revive him.

Delightful consciousness!

It brought to life and light my whole nature:

in his presence I thoroughly lived;

and he lived in mine.

~ CHARLOTTE BRONTË
JANE EYRE

e as considerate and good to me
as you were, and tell me we are friends."

"We are friends," said I, rising and bending over her,
as she rose from the bench.

"And will continue friends apart," said Estella.

I took her hand in mine,
and we went out of the ruined place;
and, as the morning mists had risen long ago
when I first left the forge,
so, the evening mists were rising now,
and in the broad expanse of tranquil light
they showed to me, I saw no shadow
of another parting from her.

~ CHARLES DICKENS
GREAT EXPECTATIONS

ild nights – wild nights!
were I with thee
wild nights should be
our luxury!

Futile – the winds –
to a heart in port –
done with the compass –
done with the chart!

Rowing in Eden –
Ah, the sea!
Might I but moor – tonight –
in thee!

~ EMILY DICKINSON

 will make you brooches and toys for your delight

> Of bird-song at morning and star-shine at night.

I will make a palace fit for you and me

> Of green days in forests and blue days at sea.

~ ROBERT LOUIS STEVENSON

I am my

beloved's,

and my

beloved

is mine.

~ The Song of Solomon

Love is a great thing,
a great good in every way:
it alone lightens what is heavy,
and leads smoothly over all roughness,
for it carries a burden without being burdened,
and makes every bitter thing sweet and tasty.
Love wants to be lifted up, not held back by anything low...:
Nothing is sweeter than love, nothing higher, nothing fuller,
nothing better in heaven and earth....

Love keeps watch and is never unaware, even when it sleeps;
tired, it is never exhausted; hindered, it is never defeated;
alarmed, it is never afraid; but like a living flame
and a burning torch it bursts upward and blares forth....

~ THOMAS À KEMPIS

Romance thrives in beautiful, quiet settings like the garden, where there is time to enjoy one another away from everyday distractions.... Talking quietly, breathing in the achingly beautiful fragrance of the earth... the excitement of being near one another mingles with the comfort of feeling safe and cherished.

~ Emilie Barnes

 here are

quiet times of romance

and there are romantic highs

during which lovers feel alive,

full of music and poetry,

and life takes on new meaning ...

Romance is an element

of fascination and delight

that culminates in a

deep desire to experience

all of life with the one we love.

~ JOAN WINMILL BROWN & BILL BROWN

Many waters cannot quench love, neither can the floods drown it.

~ THE SONG OF SOLOMON

 e walked together in the dusk

To watch the tower grow dimly white,

And saw it lift against the sky

Its flower of amber light.

You talked of half a hundred things,

I kept each hurried word you said;

And when at last the hour was full,

I saw the light turn red.

You did not know the time had come,

You did not see the sudden flower,

Nor know that in my heart Love's birth

Was reckoned from that hour.

~ Sara Teasdale

Your hands lie open in the long fresh grass, –

The finger-points look through like rosy blooms:

Your eyes smile peace. The pasture gleams and glooms

'Neath billowing skies that scatter and amass.

All round our nest, far as the eye can pass,

Are golden kingcup-fields with silver edge

Where the cow-parsley skirts the hawthorn-hedge.

'Tis visible silence, still as the hour-glass.

Deep in the sun-searched growths the dragon-fly

Hangs like blue thread loosened from the sky: –

So this winged hour is dropped to us from above.

Oh! Clasp we to our hearts, for deathless dower,

This close-companioned inarticulate hour

When twofold silence was the song of love.

~ DANTE GABRIEL ROSSETTI

There's romance
enough at home,
without going
half a mile for it;
only people
never think of it.

~ CHARLES DICKENS

To his love

Come live with me and be my love,
    And we will all the pleasures prove
That hills and valleys, dales and fields,
    Or woods or steepy mountain yields.

And we will sit upon the rocks
    And see the shepherds feed their flocks
By shallow rivers, to whose falls
    Melodious birds sing madrigals.

And I will make thee beds of roses
    And a thousand fragrant posies
A cap of flowers, and a kirtle
    Embroidered all with leaves of myrtle.

A gown made of the finest wool
    Which from our pretty lambs we pull;
Fair-lined slippers of the cold,
    With buckles of the purest gold.

A belt of straw and ivy buds
    With coral clasp and amber studs:
And if these pleasures may thee move,
    Come live with me and be my love.

The shepherd swains shall dance and sing
    For thy delight each May morning:
If these delights thy mind may move,
    Then live with me and be my love.

~ CHRISTOPHER MARLOWE

Love is quick, sincere,

dutiful, joyous, and pleasant;

brave, patient, faithful, prudent,

serene, and vigorous;

and it never seeks itself.

For whenever we seek ourselves,

we fall away from love.

Love is watchful, humble, and upright;

not weak or frivolous,

or directed toward vain things;

temperate, pure, steady, calm,

and alert in all senses.

~ THOMAS À KEMPIS

With a quick and eager step did Robin pass through the glades, for he was going to see the lady he loved best in all the world. Fair Marian was she called, the daughter of Richard FitzWalter of Malaset. Ever since when, as a boy, Robin had shot and sported in Locksley Chase, near where he had been born, Marian had been his playmate, and though she was an earl's daughter, and Robin was but a yeoman and not rich, they had loved each other dearly, and sworn that neither would marry anyone else.

~ HENRY GILBERT
ROBIN HOOD

The heart is

a living museum.

In each of its galleries,

no matter how

narrow or dimly lit,

preserved forever...

are our moments

of loving

and being loved.

~ DIANE ACKERMAN

Paintings

Morning Dogwood	Brookside Hideaway
Sweetheart Cottage III	Blessings of Spring
The Miller's Cottage, Thomashire	Stepping Stone Cottage
Autumn at Ashley's Cottage	Beside Still Waters
Heather's Hutch	Julianne's Cottage
Emerald Isle Cottage	Petals of Hope
Sweetheart Cottage II	Blessings of Autumn
Hollyhock House	Evening at Swanbrooke, Thomashire
Meadowood Cottage	Morning Glory Cottage
Pine Cove Cottage	Candlelight Cottage